Climbing Out Of Hell

A Collection of Mindsets

By
C.L. HARMON

CLIMBING OUT OF HELL
A Collection of Mindsets

© Copyright 2022 by C.L. Harmon

Printed in the United States of America

The cover of this book tells a story. It's the same story the words on the pages tell. Hell is on the back cover and on the front cover is a way out. We all create metaphorical hells in which we exist from time to time and sometimes indefinitely when we can't find our way out. The Mindsets in this book are insights that help us to find our way out of these hells on earth that we all find ourselves in. In essence, they are steps leading us out of the darkness and to the light. These are the steps leading us out of hell.

A very special thanks to Jennifer Wingfield for her valuable insight and editing skills and to Nathan Johns for his cover illustrations.

The true genius of a man lies in the madness he can control. And it is within that little control, he must keep the madness from consuming the genius of man.
- C.L. HARMON

Failure is a choice we make when we no longer wish to try. Trying is a choice we make when we no longer wish to fail. Fate is the outcome when we have no choice but to prevail. Faith is knowing that whatever the choices, our steps are never taken alone, especially when we fail.

Often the wall that your back is up against is not there to stop you from moving forward. It's there to keep someone on the other side of it from reaching you. Obstacles in your way are many times the solution to future problems that you will never know you would've had.

Civilization isn't technology and advancements in the quality of life. It is the simple act of being civil to each other. It is the principles of human nature being respected without intimidation and goodness triumphing over evil. Civilization is multiple acts of love and respect prevailing in a time and place when hatred and contempt are justifiable and desirable.

Emotions stir inside us because we feel with everything that makes us whole. We get to experience what can't be explained; we grow inside and out because the energy inside us interacts with everything we encounter. So, live without fear and restraint because every action brings new sensations that weave into our souls. And it those sensations which define our existence.

The spark inside you is controlled by you. It can either remain a tiny spark of warmth in the darkness or grow into a large passionate blaze. It will spread into all aspects of your life if you add fuel or remain insignificant if you choose to not fan its flames.

Passion is not naturally limited, but a desire that we either ignore or cultivate. And when we reach our end, it will either be the embers from a once burning blaze which warm us or the cold darkness of regrets into which we fade.

Sometimes we're given only what we need because when we're given all we want, we lose sight that it costs something to receive anything when it must come from nothing.

No matter how fast you thrust yourself forward, you will not see into the future. And no matter how much you long for the past, you will never see it again. The importance has always been now. Yesterday belongs to no one any longer and tomorrow to only those fortunate enough to be a part of it. So, right now is everything - everything you can possibly create from it before yesterday takes it from you, and tomorrow decides if you are worthy of receiving it.

What we seek in this life is often about filling a void and not about building something new. Filling a void is a repair for something in the past. Building something new is letting go of the past and creating the new life our heart knows we deserve.

Giving up is blindness by choice. By refusing to trudge forward because something is difficult, we are opting not to see what could be. Willful blindness is willful ignorance because we are choosing not to acknowledge that everything else that can ever be lies in the next step we are willing to take in faith.

Sometimes freedom is only a decision away. The life we seek waits for us to reach it because if it were to come to us, we may not recognize it. Our sought-after life contains our combined desires. And it knows that for us to recognize it, we must first choose which of our desires rest within the life we decide for ourselves.

The last step you take before you fall is only the last for that journey. The very next step you take is the beginning of a new one. We tend to see failure at a journey's end when in fact, a fall is nature's way of telling us there is something greater for us in a new direction. Our falls do not define us; they direct us.

There are those who will lend you a hand when you have fallen into a hole. They will extend a reach or throw you a rope to pull you out. But until you are ready in heart and mind to be free from the depths which hold you, the efforts to free you will always be just out of reach.

Pain has a memory. It remembers; it protects. And though it may subside and lay dormant within, it never leaves us. This is so we learn and always remember that every decision we make should be made with the mind in conjunction with the heart.

If we don't look past what we want, we may never know what we truly need. Just because something fills a void does not mean it's what is best for us. Sometimes it's better to say no or walk away from a small desire so we are not blinded to see the great ones up ahead.

If the distance you are willing to travel to meet someone on an emotional level matters more to you than the other person, then their middle is somewhere you cannot travel to without a cost to yourself. Tread lightly because their middle may be your end.

Relationships are built by adding more to what has already been put into place. But we often put off building because we feel we lack all the materials to complete. What we fail to realize though, is that the heart does not need to have everything in place to begin building. It already knows what's meant to be will make its way on its own.

If we scatter stones randomly over an area, we erect nothing. But combine them, and we can build whatever we imagine. Life is about building with what is substantial while allowing the debris to scatter into the corners of nowhere. Once we learn this, we have laid the foundation for building a better life.

Internal conflicts happen within us because we desire something that we question in our hearts being good for us. And yet our desire for what we feel we want is so strong, it seems right. But still, we have doubts. This conflict, however, is our answer to what path we should follow. Its existence alone tells us that the greatest path for us always leads to our hearts, and not the desires which lead us away from it.

———————————

Sometimes we must feel our way through moments in life. There are not always road maps and instructions to gain our bearings because where we need to go is uncharted territory. Feeling our way through is completely letting go of everything that makes sense, and still taking a step into the unknown, believing we have a place in it.

———————————

Faith is reaching for something because we believe we are supposed us to have it. Fear is not reaching for something because we believe it's not meant to be. Reaching without thought of either gives power to faith while erasing the fears which keep us from fulfillment.

———————————

We all build prisons for ourselves. Some are maximum security because we convict ourselves for life. Others are medium security because we know at some point, we need to forgive ourselves. And still others are minimum security because we realize that our mistakes do not define us; and we deserve a second chance.

———————————

Protect yourself but remain free to make mistakes. Guard your heart, but loan it those you believe worthy. Stand your ground, but always make it in the middle. Challenge your struggles and forgive the ones who trespass upon you. Recognize fear, then find the courage to ask its intent. Trust in what you can be, and always doubt those who do not share that faith.

We often seek a path riddled with obstacles. We go against what is natural, even going backwards, only to arrive at places we don't wish to be. Just because we desire something does not mean it's our path. Resistance is often nature's way of telling us we are on the wrong path. The path of least resistance guides us effortlessly to where we should go.

Sometimes there is nothing to say. Other times, there are words which must be said. And many times, we don't speak when we should and do when we shouldn't. But in each instance, it is an interaction which either connects or divides. What we convey to others either builds bridges to connect or canyons to separate. So always speak your words as though they are the ones you will be remembered by.

Diving into unknown deep water is believing that whatever lies beneath is worth experiencing. The chance that you may not resurface is what keeps you in shallow waters. But the amount of fear you are willing to overcome is not in the water, but in your desire to know your own depth.

The days you are given are not meant to be filled; they are yours to be fulfilled. Each day has a purpose which you are tasked to discover. Within that purpose is an answer you seek, a thought you need to move forward, or a new direction your life should go. Enlightenment exists in the purpose, not the trivial.

If you can live your life as though you are connected to everyone else, then every avenue in their lives becomes a new possible path for you to explore. If you choose not to, then every direction you go becomes a one-way dead end. Our connections to each other are what open the roads to new destinations.

The hell you build for yourself is only as strong as your faith allows it to be. The same stones used to build your hell can become the stepping stones out of it. Keep your faith in hand as the key to open what you believed to be the impenetrable door which kept you locked away.

Giant stones are worn down with water, steel turns to rust, and mighty trees fall in the wind. These are visions of strength which are eventually reduced to rubble. We are shown these in nature so we may realize there should never be a question that the greatest of our troubles in life, no matter how powerful, will find their way into simple dust.

Your misery exists because it doesn't know not to. Your peace is elusive because it has no direction. Your understanding is lacking because it is not fed wisdom. There are so many things in life to desire. But without the knowledge to comprehend the fundamentals of happiness, we will never understand the value of our desires, even if we obtain them.

Our actions are seeds we plant throughout our lives. And as those seeds take root and grow, they begin to spread and grow into other peoples' lives. Anger grows into thorny underbrush that overtakes fertile lands. Deceit grows into poison weeds which choke out the beauty of lush pastures. Kindness grows fragrant flowers with a scent that is carried to others in the breeze. And love grows gardens which provide what sustains us. Plant only those seeds for others which produce that which entices you enough to pick for yourself.

Finding your way in this life is not about taking all the right roads and following the directions. It's about getting so utterly lost that the only way out is to build a new road. Every known path was once a wilderness that had to first be traveled by a lost soul. And every destination at the end of those new roads was where they considered themselves found.

The easy way to anything was used up a long time ago. This leaves us with the hard way or the belief there is no way. Either way we choose, the universe will let us. And in the end, there will be no doubt as to which one we chose. Because those of us who chose the hard way will have a history admired and bewildered by those who believed there was no way.

A new beginning does not come because there is a new day or a new opportunity. It is possible because we build it. Circumstances are either invitations into something different or excuses to remain the same. The ability to change our lives resides in our willingness to move forward when everything in our current situation pulls us back.

———————

Weathering the storm does not mean you will not get wet in the pouring rain or lose your possessions to the fierce winds. It does not mean you will always be safe and sheltered from the hail and lightning. It means you are willing to carry on in its aftermath having the courage to believe that the beauty of tomorrow is greater than the carnage of today. It's the absolute acknowledgement that there is no storm more intense than the ones we create when we choose to overcome.

———————

There is something inside you clawing to get out, and you are unknowingly its prison. It may be hope, or passion, or even the truth. And only you hold the key to let it out. Every day what is locked up inside yearns for freedom. And within its release resides the element your life has been missing. Opening your heart opens your mind. And any open door is the first step to freedom.

———————

When we feel something passionately, it changes us profoundly. It's as though an energy source has been released inside us that cannot be harnessed. It is an intensity that is rare due to its overwhelming effect. And it comes with purpose that must be realized. Passion without purpose is wind in a bottle with no escape, but passion with purpose is conviction in in an unstoppable motion.

———————

There's glory in the difficult and conviction in the complicated. So many situations in life seem to test us with unwarranted difficulties. And to make it worse, they often seem like such futile tests. But it's not so much about the experiences as where they lead us. When we need a new perspective, it's not so much the route which guides us there that is important, but the enlightenment which awaits us when we get to the destination.

At times what appears to us so easy, to others seems almost impossible. We, at times, find ourselves somewhat judgmental as to why something is difficult for them. But our perspectives do not give us a full understanding into others' purpose. As such, we should always remember that the natural tools others are given and not given are intentionally beyond our understanding so we can learn to be understanding of others.

It's okay to bring remnants of yesterday into today. But only bring the pieces that help you appreciate the now and entice the anticipation of tomorrow. Everything else is already spent and should remain only in our wisdom and memories.

Being out of a negative situation is standing on the outside looking inside. It's a perspective like no other. The pain no longer has a hold on us, and the misery is falling away. But when we see it with anger, we are still connected to the negativity regardless of how far outside we may be. And that connection keeps us from finding a new inside perspective that fulfills us to the point that we never want to be on the outside again.

Letting go of everything is like free falling from a great height. But if all we do is worry about where we land, then we have only let go to grasp onto something else. Falling is our freedom because it means we hold onto nothing, and nothing holds on to us. And though it may be a hard landing, there will be no weight to carry once we pick ourselves up to move into a direction free of everything which held us in place.

So many people seek to find themselves. And if ever they find what they seek, then how sad that is for them. Because never again will they know the joy of self-discovery. We should never seek an end to what can be, when the possibilities of what could be always remain endless.

There will be those who question your intelligence. And those who second guess your choices. And even those who believe they are above you. But what they think goes no further than their own mind. Their thoughts hold no more power than yours. And if your thoughts are focused on you as much as theirs are directed towards you, then you have already proven they are wrong.

It is not just the end of a journey that should be celebrated, but also the beginning. When we begin a quest, we are taking a risk, opening ourselves up to discovery and leaving behind the fear that keeps our lives stagnant and our hearts still.

Sometimes what we chase in our lives stems from not understanding what joy there is in simplicity. We go after what is grand, with the belief it holds more than the simple that is within reach. But the reality is that one does not hold more than the other. They just each contain a different value for us. To sacrifice one for the other is never a gain because it takes both to realize the value of the other.

The shadow we cast can stretch beyond our comprehension. As such, we must acknowledge that at some point others will stand in that shadow. In essence, we are between the light and those in the shadow which we have created. The choice for us is to be the representation of the darkness in which they are standing at that moment, or the light ahead which awaits them once they move beyond our shadow.

Stop searching for answers to questions not yet ready to be asked. Cease from seeking that which is not meant to be yours. Put an end to chasing what is always outside your grasp. Misery finds you because it follows that which disappoints you. Goodness will eventually find your grasp. And then the time will be at hand for questions to be asked and answered.

Humanity should never attempt to see beyond God's veil, to know what is behind the curtain. Instead, we should just enjoy the show. The reason aspects of creation are hidden is so we may revel in the mystery and not get lost in the mundane. Spend your life being the mystery and the world will follow to watch your show.

Standing our ground should be a firm stance when defending our principles. But do not confuse them with pride. Principles are not fleeting thoughts based on emotion, but hardened ideals cultivated from life experiences. Pride, however, is just the idea of how we believe the world should act according to us.

You are of more value than you can imagine. Any negativity you see in yourself is only a minuscule part of you. Your creation is so multi-faceted that you will never realize what others see, nor completely know the impact you have on them. Live always as though you are the breath others require to survive. Because what your existence provides to others may just be exactly that.

A moment can be wasted or spent wisely. And though it may only be a moment in all of time, within it exists opportunity, salvation, freedom, and enlightenment. It is the one currency that has unlimited value. And when we realize that worth, we finally understand that a worthwhile life can be lived in the few moments we are given and realized in the single moment we accept it.

Every day we should bury our dead. With each new sunset, we should reflect upon the previous hours and know we have bid farewell to that which has died in our lives. We should never allow the spirits of yesterday to become ghosts which haunt us today. Cover that with dirt which drains the zeal from your life and plant within that soil that which is born to give you the most out of life.

Falling apart is just falling together into a new creation. And yes, it's painful. Crashing through barriers often is. But what is being created is something that has never been in existence. Your despair and despondency are the new pieces to a different you. Don't worry about holding yourself together, but instead focus on falling into a better version of you.

―――――――

Stand up today for what you hold sacred. Remind those who trespass against you that your principles carry more weight than their actions and opinions. Each time you rise after a fall is a silent statement that you tower over those who sink low enough to strike at your feet to bring you down. And it is from that height that you will walk away from those who spend their efforts crawling after you.

―――――――

Some people do things their own way because that is the only way which makes sense to them. And others will question their choices because they make no sense to them. But it only takes one person to create a new way no one thought possible. And that new way comes to fruition because, to that one person, it seemed the only way.

―――――――

You can't stop someone else's darkness, even though you may be the light. Nor are you required to own it. The misery which swallows them is not yours to taste. To overcome the gloom which inhabits them, they must only use your light to illuminate how they create their own. But you should never allow them to take your light to feed their darkness.

―――――――

Finding fault is like finding fools' gold. It has little or no value. Placing blame solves nothing, nor does it open a door to a new direction. Accepting fault when it is due, however, is a treasure chest of pure gold. When we accept what diminishes us, we change and grow into our worth. And when we do not assess blame on others, be it their fault or not, we give them an opportunity to seek their own treasure and increase their self-worth.

Our strengths define us because they are born out of weakness. It is in the struggle to overcome where we find integrity. It's in what's difficult and tempting that forces us to fight against what we know is wrong. It is in our broken and fragile states where we are too weak to fight that we learn to forgive. And it is in our desperation that we to opt to persevere and not perish. Every weakness we have is simply a future strength we have yet to cultivate.

Reside in your mind and you will discover that all roads have destinations. But follow your heart and it will lead you on endless journeys your mind cannot even fathom.

Goodness is inherent; it's recognizable. We feel it when we see it. But that which is less righteous is often disguised and cunning. And those who wear such masks and practice deception often use the shadows from the light to mimic good intentions. So, if what you feel on the inside about someone needs a candle to be identified, ask yourself why it is you can't feel the warmth of their light.

The cold winds of reality chill to the bone, and the storms in life knock the wind out of us because suffering teaches us that everything on this side of life has a cost. Only through payment of what hurts to lose can we treasure the gains we are fortunate to hold. And may we all love enough that to lose what we held is an unbearable cost reimbursed in faith on the other side of life.

In life, remember yesterday as though your dreams were achieved. Fight today as though only a victory will bring about tomorrow. Live always as though happiness is in every next step ahead of you. And in dying, know you lived it right.

There will be those who come close to destroying you. But each day you survive tears a little away at their intent. Their willingness to break you down erodes against your determination to stand up. Your resolve is the only weapon from which there is no defense and the only one you need to rise above them.

The unique design of this life always offers us a natural compass. We can choose to go in any direction we wish to explore. And occasionally those directions render us lost. But as with a compass where there is a sense of consistent direction, life always provides a way out, a direction for hope. But to find it, we must trust in the belief that as lost as we may be, we have never gone so far that there is no other way.

Life isn't about fair or unfair; it's about purpose. And that purpose supersedes all else because it is connected to the soul. We are born with it and created for it. But that purpose is a lifelong endeavor, which ultimately means that we, at times, may perceive our lives as being unfair due to being directed in areas we feel we don't wish to go. However, if we understood what impact that purpose has on humanity, we would be in awe as to how little of a sacrifice we were required to give for such an incredible contribution to the betterment of God's creation.

Monsters are real. They are under the bed and in the closet, in the dark and the light. Feelings such as rage, revenge, hate, and fear create them every day. And the nature of a monster is to destroy peace, forgiveness, love, and security. In essence, the monsters we create are the monsters we become. But the ones we acknowledge and destroy transform us into what they would have ravaged.

Sometimes we are required to stand alone. This is because there are battles in life that only we are equipped to defend. And as frightening as that may seem, doesn't the idea that we are given a strength unique to each of us for defeating that which attacks us individually also mean there is no collective enemy we cannot conquer when we stand together?

There will be days in our lives when we are blind because where we are going must be led by someone else. There will be hours we are deaf because what is being spoken around us is detrimental to our purpose. There will be moments when we are without a voice because our words may destroy more than build. There will be seconds we are utterly lost without direction because it is the responsibility of others to find us. But it is because of these absences we become whole. Without them, we are fragments of our choices void of faith, the sixth sense which connects us to our Creator.

Whatever we want in this life will cost. To gain anything requires something from us. Wisdom has been paid with mistakes, knowledge has been paid with hard work, experience has been paid with failure and faith has been paid with desperation. This is the law of nature which teaches us to gain something without costs is to have gained nothing at all.

We are not redeemed because others accept the belief we have been redeemed. True redemption is only offered divinely in spirit and by self-choice in flesh. Forgive yourself even when others will not. Because not even for one second will they ever wear your burdens.

Seek that which will take root and will hold when the winds rage. Chasing anything which constantly moves means we are more engaged in catching than in constructing. That which takes root has roamed until it found the optimal conditions in which to grow. It has done so because in its journey, it discovered that the wind always controlled its fate until it chose to stand tall against it.

Every single day is different. The sun rises and sets the same and much of it is filled with routine. But each day has the opportunity for a new growth that was not there the previous day. This is because we are building upon yesterday's opportunities we choose to seize. And it's within those opportunities our new hope in each tomorrow is created.

There will be countless activities we will not see, hear, or experience today. These processes will surround us and be close to us, but we will not acknowledge their existence. Because the pursuit of responsibility and structure is our definition of sanity, we become oblivious to the magic around us. But this beauty cares not for such pursuits of responsibility, but only to exist and be recognized. So, every now and then, seek out your insanity and let the small countless miracles around you become your reality.

The greatest adventure is seeking what we desire. No matter how small our desire, the journey to it is where we feel most alive. The outcome is the reward, but it is only a reflection at the end of the road. So, with each step today, embrace your failures, allow your laughter to engulf you, let your tears puddle and your victories humble you. And in the end, that reflection will be the inspiration others will utilize on their adventures.

Responsibility is a word, a simple word, that has a never-ending meaning. It's a combination of letters encompassing everything in life. No matter your beliefs, status, or race, you are affected by responsibility, that which you accept and that accepted by others. When we fail in our responsibilities, we fail others in the present and ourselves in the future. In essence we become either accomplishments or excuses. And that outcome is the result of another simple word - choice.

It should matter not whether our leaders conduct themselves in a Godly manner. It should only matter that those who trust in God conduct themselves in a manner which shows God is their first leader. He, as the first among many, will always subdue the few who lead and believe themselves above the many.

It's easy to buy a lie because the truth is a much harder sell. It's easier to marry a mistake than to make amends. It's more fun to dance with the devil than kneel before the Lord. It's safer to fall than rise; and it's acceptable to be accused but not vindicated. We live on a shifting, splitting, bedrock of weakness. Solid, stable ground is hard and uncompromising. As such, we avoid building lasting structures. If your world is falling apart beneath your feet, perhaps it's time to find harder ground on which to stand.

Life is an experience in worth where the income is often less than the outcome, but the value always outweighs the cost.

To have integrity will alienate you from those with a willingness to sacrifice their morals. But remember that a seed is covered with dirt, drowned in water, hidden from the sunlight, and left to dwell in darkness. And yet it takes everything that is seemingly against it and uses them to reach up and break through the ground. To have honor in a world rampant with immortality is to be the seed that grows tall above the weeds which attempted to choke it out.

If we give up part of ourselves for what is immoral or selfish, we have sold our souls to become slaves to a master. As such, we do their bidding no matter the cost to others. Freedom is gained and kept on battlefields, but before a single bullet is fired, we must be free in our minds and selfless in our hearts. Those who realize this understand that the nature of a master is to control, while the requirement of a slave is to obey. The righteous already know this and further, that regardless of what is gained by the slave, the right to utilize it will always belong to the master.

Fear robs you of what is rightfully yours. And when it finishes stealing, it leaves regret as a reminder of all you lost and all you could have gained.

We all tie ourselves to anchors. We are tied to that which keeps us in a realm we choose to exist. However, we must choose wisely as some anchors can act as prisons keeping us from roaming, while others are simply a security allowing us to explore with a sense of peace that we are tethered to something strong, regardless of how far we go.

Embrace that which forces you to let go of your darkness, and allow that which has crumbled in your life to return to dust. Do not build new foundations for the future in the blackness of the past where there is no light, and do not use the rubble from it as the base to build the walls.

Free will causes collateral damage. It's the freedom to hurt others or to help them, to save or condemn them. And because of its powerful nature, we are given a heart, mind, and soul to ensure we use it wisely. But when any of these elements are ignored, the collateral damage will eventually reach its way back to the free will which spurred it.

Allow yourself to wither and die a little each day so that tomorrow will have room to add a new idea, a new experience, a new love. Often what we keep alive on the inside doesn't allow space for what we desire on the outside.

Everything you want is on the side of difficulty, the inside of chaos, the backside of failure. So, trip and fall with pride, crawl without regret, and claw with a jovial attitude to reach it. Because when you do reach your destination, you will have not only found what you want, but also realized it was the journey you actually needed.

Desire is the key in a world with many locks, and passion leads us to the correct lock. But growth and wisdom are what tell us when we are ready to unlock it. Opening something before we are ready to receive it often makes blessings seem like curses. As such, we are to practice patience which is the keychain that we carry our passion and desire on until we are ready to experience what had been locked away from us.

Often the road you're on is long, arduous, and seemingly without relevant purpose. But somewhere along that road is a purpose you would never understand had you not suffered the journey. And that purpose is to understand that the road you're on was built just for you because there was no other road available for you to get to the destination you desire.

In the sky we call them clouds, but on the ground, we know it as fog. Although it's the same, we see it differently, we name it differently. Because we see it differently, it becomes something different to us. We do this with other aspects in life as well. But the essence of a cloud remains the same regardless of where it is located. The same is true of us. As such, we should always remember the essence of humanity is goodness, and then realize that others' negative actions and demeanor aren't about us, but where they are in life.

Whatever you do in this life, own it. Good or bad, call it yours and take it wherever you go. It's not about the pride you feel or shame you wish to escape at the moment. It's about the growth, the lesson, the experience. Running changes nothing. Though you can leave it, it never leaves you. So, accept that which you create, and it will allow you to create the life you wish to own.

The key to life is knowing how to live it. Do not waste your youth on ideals that you are not ready yet to understand. Learn to accept that what is out of your control is for your own good. Fail with grace because failing without it makes you appear weak. Love hard and let go peacefully. Laugh when it hurts and smile when you lose. And in the end, feel blessed to have had the greatest experience that you would never want to do again.

The reason we are often at a standstill in life is because there is something we are not seeing, and we cannot move forward until it is revealed to us. Although the direction in which we move is a choice, the timing for it is divine. So do not fret when you feel idle, but gather hope that when the timing is right, you will have been given enough time to choose the best direction.

The idea that others' words and opinions should affect our feelings is not a law written in stone. It is simply a choice as to how we will allow them to make us feel. What is often lost is the knowledge that we have all the power. By simply not allowing others to affect us in a way we don't like is an aspect of free will. By refusing to be affected, we become empowered by our choice to be free of it.

When our influences on the outside become stronger than our faith on the inside, we have stepped into dangerous territory. Listening to others does often feed our growth. But believing in ourselves is the voice of the divine telling us we can be more than anyone on the outside can even fathom.

Our connections to others are living legacies which affect us daily. Our interactions are seeds planted in their souls. As long as we live, we are sowing into and reaping from the lives of others. Once we understand this, we realize that most of what we harvest comes from the fields of others.

I don't so much believe bad things happen for a reason as I believe they happen because of our bad choices to not use reason.

As we age, our objective should not only be to grow up and accept growing older, but to grow forward. In doing so, we will learn not to laugh at someone, but with someone. To cry with someone and not for someone. To follow through and not fall through, and to lose ourselves so we can be found by others who are lost. Growing forward means never looking back with the regret of not growing up.

Wanting change in our lives is about effort. It's about working and not wishing. It's true that things in life change because of universal momentum, but without effort we give that change no direction. We are given the distinction of navigating our lives through free will. We are also victims of that momentum when we opt to not provide guidance. Work toward the change you want, and the universe will step aside as you lead the way.

There is hope. And it lies in the belief that everyone is beautiful to someone. There is passion. And it is for you burning in the heart of another. There is peace. And it's in every soul that has witnessed a world without it. There is light. And it is illuminated by only you, making you someone's brightest moment. There is kindness. It's for you and finds you when the bitter chill of hatred clutches. Then there is you. And within that unique and purposeful creation you will learn you are someone's everything.

What we seek is never far from us. God never puts our desires very far out of reach. He does, however, expect us to take a step or two in faith, reach blindly into a new direction, dream a vision into reality and step up when all else is falling away to reach those desires. Each of these can be extensive journeys - this is true, but none of these ever lead us away from His grasp and the desires He is holding for us to discover.

Each new day is a gift. Our quest is to figure out how to open it. Once we do, we learn that the significance of the gift is exactly what we need today. When our moods and current situations put us in a mindset that our day is a burden, we minimize the value of the gift before we even know its contents. And that is an entire day lost to what will be instead of what could be.

Choices are links in a chain. The hope is that most will be strong links which help us extend the length of our chain as we move forward through life. Each new link offers us more options in which to utilize our chain. But if we are not careful, we will add weak links which eventually break, cutting off anything below it. And the shorter the chain, the fewer uses which are available to us.

You must not only wait for a miracle but work toward it and trust that it exists just beyond your reach. When time is running out or you are tired and too weak to give one more minute of labor to your journey, you will find the miracle knew you before your journey even began. And it was waiting to carry you the rest of the way.

When you figure out where you don't want to be, you're on your way to where you wish to go. In the meantime, make the effort to realize where you're supposed to be. Then you will always be traveling away from where you shouldn't be, and always be enroute to where you need to be.

It's not about choosing the right door or the wrong door, but about what you do with what you find on the other side. Why worry about which path we take when everyone has its challenges? Expect the difficult, challenge the disappointments, and embrace the resolve it takes to overcome. Because then and only then will you know all that you can conquer.

Our lives can change in a moment. From upside down to right side up and vice versa, we are pulled into the storm or released into the gentleness of the calm. One is to release us and the other to enlighten us. But the significance of that change is hope. It means that we never stay the same. And with that is the never-ending opportunity to seek what makes us happy and become who we desire to be.

There will be those days when everything just seems to go wrong. But beneath the wrong, hidden within the chaos of those days is the experience. And within that is knowledge, wisdom, awaiting memories, and the opportunity for perseverance. Accepting what is beyond our control as a valuable addition equal to that which is in our control, balances us to the point where everything we encounter adds to a life where experiences become our most valued treasures.

So much of what we give value to in this world is not found on the surface but buried deep beneath us. Gemstones, oil, freshwater, and precious metals must all be sought out from the depths. And knowing this, we still often fail to see what is hidden deep within each other. We seek very little past the surface. And yes, it takes effort and patience to reach the depths. But this, it seems, is nature's way of teaching us that what we value most is formed on the inside and rewarded to those willing to seek it from the depths.

Part of our journey is losing ourselves. Being off course holds answers just as the beaten path does. We are not always meant to know where we are and what direction we are going. Sometimes what we need most is found in the wilderness. Often, being lost in the thick dense no man's land is our only opportunity to look inside ourselves and find the directions we need to move on the outside.

Whatever you feel, be that without haste. Whatever your appearance, wear it. Whatever the voice in your head, listen to it. Whatever the tune in heart, dance to it. Feeling these is your soul revealing who you should be - who you need to be to change the world and make it yours.

Finding our way seems to imply we may be lost. When, in fact, it usually means just finding other ways. If we are not seeking new paths, then we truly will become lost. We are always on some path, but new ones exist because they are meant to take us to new understandings. Seeking anything is not an indication we are off course, but proof we are enlightened enough to know that it often takes many paths to find the destination to which we belong.

It's true that what we lose may never be returned to us. However, our emphasis seems to be on what we had as not having an equal, and thus being an ending of sorts. And perhaps that's true. But life doesn't work in a tit-for-tat format. Each person and each experience have its own value unlike anything else created. As such, it's not so much that we are losing something irreplaceable, but instead moving forward to seek something else that is in a world of never-ending experiences.

A moment in time, a moment of great significance and light. It's there and then it's gone. This is life with its past moments like ghosts haunting what was and unable to move forward. We too become these ghosts trapped within time when we view what was as being better than what can be. But letting go of those moments allows time to push our hearts and minds into what awaits us, while staying in the past leaves us as only aging shadows left to yesterday's light.

Free will is our choice to live with a closed fist or a free hand. Holding onto negativity is like clutching stones. They have no value other than to hurl them at others. They become heavy over time and leave no space to carry anything else. But when we let them go, we then have the option to pick up anything we desire, including the hand of those for whom we once held rocks.

Faith is not about taking the right road every time, but about believing its destination will lead to fulfillment, regardless of how long we must travel it or our doubts that it may not have been the best road in the beginning.

You are a miraculous creature. Despite your faults, failures, and shortcomings and because of your gifts, talents, and accomplishments, you have evoked emotions in others, impacted the planet, altered the world, and resided in the thoughts of others. So, the next time negative thoughts of self-worth overtake you, remember that the miracle you need to overcome arrived the day your existence was conceived.

In a world where everything is for sale, be the one who offers freely. When everyone else is taking, be the one who is giving. Be what everyone else is not. Do what no one else wants to do. Stand alone when others follow. In doing so, all eyes will be upon you, and you will be the one who sees amid a crowd of the blind. You will become the light which restores the sight of those who have never experienced life as seen through their own eyes.

The universe listens. We are intertwined within it and therefore connected and tethered to it. It works by design to guide us and support us. But it only responds to positivity because that is what it recognizes. It doesn't know what to do with negativity. It was created to help move us forward, not backwards. It returns positivity when we put it into the world. But with negative energy, it senses only emptiness and therefore has nothing to return.

They both share passion, conviction of their beliefs, drive, and a desire to change. One is a tyrant and the other a saint. They are the same tools to reach very different objectives. They are paths which run parallel but end in opposite destinations. And with all their similarities, there is but one major distinction. It's the choice to place oneself above others or others above oneself. Each is a key for us to open our life experiences. One unlocks the door to our heaven and the other to our hell.

If you view your life as an opportunity for God to do something that can only be done through your existence, your life instantly has purpose. No matter your mistakes and failures, you have an objective which equates to value. Getting lost in the chaos of life doesn't affect this purpose. Never judge your value by the way the world causes you to feel, but instead by the accomplishment of a purpose that could've only happened because of you.

Sometimes the only freedom you can give yourself is letting go. There are certainly times on which to hold. But when your grip becomes so intense that it becomes painful to both you and what you are clutching, any relief or security you were gaining has gone. Prison walls are built one stone at a time with each one holding you a bit more in place. Freedom is acquired with a single full blow from a wrecking ball that has been released.

Fear and respect work hand in hand. We fear others when they have authority over us, but when that control is utilized to teach and empower us, it transforms into respect. Everything in life needs something else to make it complete. Alone, nothing has balance. And without balance, harmony cannot exist. Fear is only the beginning of respect which was not nurtured into respect. The same is true with kindness, which becomes progress when combined with direction. Seek all the necessary elements in your endeavors and the results will always be harmonious.

Everything was once an abyss. What is comfortable and civilized now was once a dark chaos. It took desire, willpower, and effort to bring it light and order. This is what we are tasked with in life. What is already tamed are examples that bringing light is always possible despite the depths of the darkness. Your life is your turn to tame more of the wilderness so those after you will have a place to stand before conquering their own abyss.

The problem with someone else determining your worth is that they have no idea how much has been invested in you by God. He values your existence enough to have created you. Once you realize that, it makes the value others have of you seem insignificant.

There will be moments in your life when you will need to be a leader, take the helm, and lead others. But always lead them to the direction which calls to them. But first it is our nature to follow as we are followers first. This is because we must learn to lead ourselves even as we follow others. Never allow yourself to be led by the will of others who only follow their own direction, or their hell may become your destination.

Sometimes we need to burn things down, torch a swath, and set parts of our past ablaze. Every civilization began in the wilderness, and as each one grows it also decays as the decrepit and worn need removed and replaced by the new. Left alone, that which crumbles and no longer has value grows back into a new wilderness. But that which is razed to the ground leaves the opportunity to build a new beginning.

Understanding your place in life means coming to terms with the pieces strewn about in your head. Finding that place means getting them out of your head and setting them in place. Realization you are where you're supposed to be is finally seeing those pieces connected to everyone else's pieces. Life is an unfinished puzzle with your small pieces making a larger piece, which then adds to a whole, bringing it closer to completion.

Do something so profoundly positive today that the universe takes notice. Do not strive to change the world with concepts of grandeur, but with a small action for one person who needs a change in their world. The universe does not care about the magnitude of the deed but only the impact. And that impact may just become someone else's profound action, that changes the world for everyone.

The weak-willed will always follow evil if it's presented as something easy or free. The strong-willed, however, lead the way to goodness because they are drawn to what is greater than themselves. And that which is greater is rarely easily attainable. Being a leader is not only just choosing not to simply follow evil; it's pursuing that which is greater with such vigor that others choose to lead with you in pursuit of the discovery you seek.

Some days you will feel defeated... and you will be. The pieces will break, and the shards will crash around you. Your bones will ache and darkness you will see from all sides. But then there will be a memory which pulls you from the day's abyss, a soothing tune or just a comfort in the closing of that day, because hope abounds. Let us never forget that hope is the greatest of creations that lives in the smallest of experiences.

Whatever it might be you are walking through today, believe that you are either moving away from something negative or toward something positive. So, walk with the grace that makes others want to walk in your direction. Walk with the courage that makes others want to follow and experience what it's like to own the path. Walk with conviction so others will step out of your way. And never give anyone the satisfaction of knowing they have the power to make you run from them.

You can view life through the smallest of perspectives if you choose. You can ignore or include whatever you wish. The levels of ignorance you possess are directly linked to the size of world you choose to learn from and experience. But know that when the world seems too large and overwhelming, it's quite possible that your perspective in life is so small because all you see is the ignorance.

The heart holds five elements: light, love, darkness, hate, and peace. Each are molded into human creation with purposeful precision for the intention of bringing about understanding. A rich man does not see as a poor man, nor does a poor man see as a rich one. We only see what we are and not what we are not. And so, we must be all elements. We are the light. Not to see, but to be the beacon. We are love. Not because we love, but because we are a part of what creates it. We are darkness. Not because we are evil, but because we are the example of what occurs when the light is shunned. We are hate. Not because we are void of love, but because we are inherently affected by the absence of it. We are peace. Not because we seek peace, but because we transform into it through acts of forgiveness.

Before stepping out of what feels like shaky ground, make sure the stability to which you are moving is solid ground. It's much easier to fight your demons on the unsteady ground of which you are familiar than the unknown depths of which they are familiar.

Chaos is not necessarily a bad thing. Sometimes life just needs to pull everything from the closets and drawers, clutter the floors with it, and lay it out in piles so it can sort out everything you have been hoarding, collecting, and storing. This happens when it's time for you to move to a new place in your life without all the baggage that has kept you in a place which no longer has purpose for you.

When the odds are stacked against you, win anyway. When your heart is torn out, pick up a needle and thread. When you've been wronged, allow being right to be your peace. When alone, get to know yourself. When you're down and out, build up and move in. When everything is out of control, control yourself. And when all else fails, make failure the burden which must carry all your successes.

One day you will realize that everything you know will no longer seem worrisome. There will be a changing of your heart and mind that seems to have come out of nowhere. Your mind will see in new directions and your heart will follow because it will be compelled. And though it's the unknown, you will explore it without fear. This is how we get from here to there. It's called growth. And it is the gift you receive for taking all the frightening steps you took into the tomorrows when you felt you had nothing left to offer.

The very essence of our existence is to experience. Everything in our world is connected through that we experience. And at times, it's painful. But you can only get experience through life. It's not available anywhere else. We become a unique entity because we experience, not because we exist. We are created in phases. In the beginning, we are born with the tools to experience, then evolve as we learn and yet continually become someone different through our experiences. So never assume your life is at a standstill. Your life is constantly in motion, creating you one experience at a time.

Sorrow swims deep, to depths we are never supposed to go. It takes us down until we are absent of breath and light. We sometimes stumble so far into the abyss; directions are useless as we become tangled within the darkness. But hope is in the light which doesn't know the darkness, and in the shallow which does not fear the deep. When you are hope, you are someone else's angel reaching in to pull them from the abyss. And that's the power which heaven has afforded to you.

Be a man with the dirt of labor on your hands, not one with the blood of those in bondage. Be a woman of strength, not of servitude. Bring a spark of hope to the future; leave the ashes of despair in the past. Stand tall to give those who cower an example. Be filled with joy; let sorrow hunger in the belly. Lead when compelled and follow the lead when your intuition compels. And always listen to your heart as it alone speaks for the soul.

The legacy you leave today is the day you define yourself. Now is when you take what was yesterday and that which you desire for tomorrow, create a new opportunity, and breathe life into any legacy you choose. Others' choices affect you for moments, but a lifetime identity is only affected by you. It is better to leave a blank epithet on stone than one carved in the regret of who you wish you had been.

We build paths to avoid obstacles. We fight the brush, boulders, and pitfalls to clear a way for ourselves and others to reach the destinations we seek. But when the expectation becomes that others will fight the obstacles and risk the dangers associated with clearing the path, new safe and secure paths remain hidden in the wilderness. Because although expectation belongs to us all, progress toward it is our own responsibility.

In life we should fill a void, and in death leave one. As part of our creation, a void only for us to fill is also created, which is part of our purpose. That void is spread through and affects the people we will encounter in life. As such, we are linked together through a connection to fill that void. And ironically, it is because of that void of nothingness that we are brought together to create unity in everything.

Hope is not in a sunrise or in a rainbow. Hope exists only in a heart of action and of faith. Injustice occurs because the just remain silent. Prejudice persists because tolerance is accepted as compromise. Evil flourishes because the faithful pray, but do not act with a will of conviction. And the weak fall to tyranny because they do not rise when tyrants shake the ground beneath their feet. Hope is, and has always been, in you. And you realize this at the foot of the cross where you can witness just what faith in action can accomplish.

There are two options in every situation: to accept or not to accept. It's that simple. Whatever situation we find ourselves in is a direct result of which one of these we choose. To believe that which befalls us is someone else's fault may provide us with a sense of understanding. But it does not absolve us of the part we play by our choice of acceptance.

It's not that we don't learn from history; it's just those with evil intent learn it better.

Defiance is not always the wrong choice. It is the right choice when tyranny is pushed. It is the right choice when freedom is oppressed. It is the right choice when you are ordered into a direction that makes your heart uneasy. The only reason free and civilized societies exist is because others stood in defiance of those who pushed self-serving agendas and called defiance civil disobedience instead of civil liberty.

Everything in life and in this world moves. It is in some process of change. This is because change is the lifeblood of existence. And that blood flows continually in a direction that is rarely the path of least resistance to push the most doors of growth open. As a result, it often seems we are not moving forward in life. In actuality, our flow has just been slowed, so we don't miss seeing the many open doors that life has afforded us.

What you lose today, you may never get back. But within that loss is a gain that has a value only you can give it. You can allow that loss to have no wisdom or knowledgeable insight. You can let anger, regret and bitterness guide you to your next life situation and then build upon them. But when those foundations crumble, remember that you built that life with what you considered the greatest value your past experiences afforded you.

Be free of expectation in heart and mind. Have faith in what is possible and confidence in that faith which makes all things possible. Life's value is not a measure of met or unrealized expectations, but a review of how yesterday's faith brought about today's opportunity to believe less in what we expect and further into the miracle of new possibilities.

When you would rather sacrifice all for what you believe in than live with nothing under the beliefs of another and love enough to be completely vulnerable and to trust again after your soul has been shattered by another, you have been awakened to the cost of every freedom that exists.

Instead of saying today is the start of a positive life, say that yesterday was the end of a negative one. Nothing in your past has control over you without your consent and declaring an end to anything from the past automatically sets up a beginning. Once you have let it go, you must only give permission to the positive to be part of that beginning.

You will never know how much you affect someone's life. Because knowing how much is not as important as believing that even the smallest of impacts is enough to change the world for them.

We reach for addictions. And they reach back with the embrace of the devil. We chase the winds of uncertainty even when we know they will carry us into storms of destruction. We drown in the misery of the saddest melodic notes that constantly play in the background. And we dance with memories while the future stands alone waiting for a new song to find us. Because we choose to travel these roads, we will ultimately become the darkness to which they lead. But the light, no matter how dim, cares not about its hold on us. It will always pull us toward it as it recognizes that even the smallest flicker in us belongs with it.

Doing what is right costs. It costs something we value, something which hurts to lose. As such, it becomes easier to hold onto what we give worth, than to let it go and invest in the greater good. And within the good that is lost is the cost we ultimately pay for placing more value on ourselves than on others. Holding onto more in hopes of losing less only has true worth if others see that value. And no one places worth on selfishness and arrogance because they gain nothing from it. They value what is gained more by others' humility and sacrifice.

If you only focus on what you can't have, all you will ever possess is what you can't have.

Control is sought by the weak-minded. Those who possess it live in fear of losing it. They become slaves to its whims just to simply wield it longer. It owns them. It is irony in constant motion, as the very power they wish to possess is the very same which holds them hostage.

Sometimes it takes everything you have just to make it through the day. But remember at the end of that day you had just enough to make it all the way through. And that's all the proof you need to know that tomorrow will never be able to take more than you must give.

There's a fine line between faith and ignorance. Faith is allowing where you are going is being directed by God. Ignorance is ending up exactly where your map directed and blaming God because you believed He was driving.

We all have a responsibility to each other to be righteous. In different capacities we are one another's judges, juries, counselors, and caregivers. If we do not practice righteousness, then those we are responsible for will always be on the short side of fairness and justice. And with no example from us, the same lack of practice will find us when we are in the care of others.

Our voices must be louder than the howl of the wolves in the wilderness. The wolves do not fear the sheep, but the cunning and intelligence of the shepherd. It only takes one wolf to be a danger to the flock. But it only takes one voice to strike hesitancy in the wolf as well. Silence is often an invitation to evil, whereas a voice from the wilderness is the protection which keeps it at bay.

Direction is a choice. Fate is a result of decisions. And destiny is when we realize God loves us more than He hates our choice of direction.

When you find mystery, follow it. When you capture desire, live it. When you discover passion, chase it. When you taste the sweet, savor it. But when you find your true self, give yourself away so that you too can become a unique experience for everyone you will ever encounter.

When you add a brush stroke to a painting or a word to a poem, you have changed it from what it is becoming to what it will be. This is exactly what you do in life with every choice you make. Create those choices which others will admire, and they will see beyond the individual strokes and words and will view the whole of your life as art worthy of imitation.

When you begin to see the color in the world as an accent to enhance beauty, differences in beliefs as entrances to open mindedness, and imperfection as the perfect method to create equality, then you have seen beyond human comprehension and into the Divine belief that hope can overcome ignorance.

You are the spark for someone else's fire. Think about what that means. Whether you are firing up, melting down or burning out, it does not matter to others who need your warmth. To them, you are the flame that made every fire they ever started possible. And that means everything to them.

The only time someone will act the way you wish they would is when acting the way you wish they would is their choice.

What you remove from your existence defines you as much as what you add to your life. Often, what you choose is not as important as what your choice leaves behind. If we choose fear, it is courage that is left behind. If we choose hatred, then love is what we leave. If we choose tyranny, liberty remains behind. And therein lies the irony that the positivity we leave behind will be an eternal reminder defining us by the negativity we chose to keep.

There are three Trinities in this world. The first is divine, and consists of the Father, the Son, and the Holy Spirit. The second is human, and consists of love, empathy, and forgiveness. And the final one is self, which consists of enlightenment, self-worth, and knowledge. Once we recognize these and apply them to our lives, the answers we seek, the ones so elusive, will find their way to us.

When we understand that everything in the universe was created perfectly and that we have the power to throw it into chaos, then we truly realize just how much responsibility is entrusted to us. Morality is easy. It's deceit which is complicated. There is only one truth but there are always countless lies to remember, organize, and manage. And though morality demands honesty and integrity from us, it is simple in the sense that it only asks from us what is owed. Deceit, however, unravels in burdensome chaos when confronted with truth, taking everything from us and still leaving us indebted to morality and those who practice it.

I hope my youth is stored away in a bottle somewhere, corked and waiting for me to release it. I hope my mistakes are sealed and locked in a distant abyss to be forgotten. I hope that all I have lost will be found along the roads I have yet to travel. And I hope that which has been broken is in the hands of the Divine. And though mine and all our hopes at times may seem unlikely to materialize, they are still the opposite of acceptance that they won't. And that reason alone is why hope exists.

Being ourselves is the only thing we will ever be perfect at. And you know what is so great about that? Being ourselves means we fail; it means we lose; it means we suffer. But above every good or bad we experience, it means we have created the only version of ourselves that will ever exist, and there's no measure above that perfection.

In this life, we tether ourselves between people who represent either Heaven or Hell. As such, both will pull at us. But it is we who choose how much of a foothold either one has. And for that we must decide which one is pulling to be with us and which one only cares to keep us from the other. One will keep us grounded; the other will drag us down.

You are given three tools necessary to achieve happiness: a brain, heart, and a conscience. When you find that you are unhappy, ask yourself which ones you are not listening to.

There is a mystery in everything. And what a dull world it would be without it. We see it in all things. As such, perhaps we are the same to our Creator; a mystery. The possibility exists that even our choices, and thus our outcomes, are perhaps a mystery the Divine keeps for Himself.

Beneath a headstone lies much more than what was. In that resting place is wisdom, knowledge and experience that is no longer accessible. This creates two responsibilities with those left behind. The first is to share what you know to help others. The second is to acknowledge that you have only a limited amount of time to utilize the help you need before it's buried.

There are those with the skill to build instruments, those with the talent to play those instruments and, those with the creativity to write the music for both. Each of us is given a gift and they all intertwine. As such, we should never envy the ability of another. Because what they do with their gift may provide exactly what we need to utilize ours.

Our creation comes with a calling. It's what we are drawn to and equipped to fulfill. It is a responsibility that we have no choice but to acknowledge. But until we see this calling as a responsibility, the purposes we are designed to fulfill will be left undone. And this is something we should all remind ourselves when we look at the world and ask why it is not the way we believe it should be.

The value others have of you matters little, if at all. No one knows your true worth but you. You can't tell others, convince them, or sell them your value. They will either know it or they won't. And if they don't, it won't matter. Because value lost to those who didn't see it weren't worth what you would have given them anyway.

Because of past scars, we tend to proceed with caution when we move toward our desires. Often, we miss or lose out on something worthwhile because we wish to control the natural rhythm inside us. Whether we move slowly or not, the possibility of failure is still real. But to lose a desire because we didn't simply follow the rhythm of our hearts is an injustice to ourselves and to that or those which we desired.

Faith is believing in purpose. When we acquire a puzzle, there are two assumptions made. The first is that all the pieces are in the box. The second is that the photo on the box will be the completed image once all the pieces are in place. In other words, we have faith that what we are constructing has reason and conclusion even when they are only still pieces scattered about in chaos. We don't question who made the puzzle or why the image of the puzzle was chosen because the connecting of the pieces is what is important. Is life no different? Aren't we just putting the pieces of our lives together to build the life we want? Instead of worrying that the chaotic mess will not fit together one piece at a time, we should trust more that the creator of those pieces made exactly the right amount of perfectly fitting pieces to build the image of the life we desire.

Faith is a double edge sword with a reversible handle. On one end, there is a handle meant for us to grasp and wield using the edge provided for us to defend that which we are capable. At other times, the handle is on the other end leaving us only the edge so we cannot grasp it. This is to teach us that not every battle is ours to fight. Some victories in this life can only be won when the handle is in the hand of the sword maker.

Allow yourself peace today. Reinvigorate your spirit today by choosing to believe in what you can't see. Whatever your situation, it is changing. And those changes are the seeds of peace. Not seeing the change does not mean there isn't growth. What is happening beneath the soil is occurring whether you believe it or not. Believing something is happening without proof of any kind is the garden from where peace grows.

Some people succumb to evil so much that they become it. They choose to embrace it instead of denying it. But whatever their actions caused by the evil they become, is they're evil and not a definition of any instrument or reasoning which they use. Never blame the light for what the darkness takes as its own, but simply let it recede into its fate. Soon the darkness of those who chose it will become so vast, they will have no access to anything in the light.

When you commit evil, it learns your name. It will remember who you are and that it can ask and expect anything of you that it so chooses. You have become a servant to weakness and mindless in your attempts to use evil as a weapon. You have given up your identity to become one with whatever evil you have allowed to own you. No matter what you gain or accomplish through your deeds, your legacy has become the weakness to which you have succumbed.

Morality is easy. It's deceit which is complicated. There is only one truth, but there are always countless lies to remember, organize and manage. And though morality demands honesty and integrity from us, it is simple in the sense that it only asks from us what is owed. Deceit, however, unravels in burdensome chaos when confronted with truth, taking everything from us and still leaving us indebted to morality and to those who practice it.

We believe in kindness even when we don't see it. We believe justice prevails when it doesn't seem to be in our courts. We find hope when hopelessness is all around us. We move forward when everything seemingly knocks us backwards. We do so because there is something inside us that evil cannot touch, a strength impervious to what wishes to destroy us. And when we believe in it, it will be that strength which leads us to what saves us.

Reason brings compromise, fairness, and justice. Reasonable violence is brought about because those who live by reason no longer wish to live without it.

Patience is a gift we offer ourselves. Happiness is a gift we give ourselves. Joy is a gift we allow ourselves. Tolerance is a gift we teach ourselves and success is a gift we define for ourselves. And within all these gifts is peace, the only one which comes because we recognize we must gift ourselves that which we wish to fulfill us.

The belief that life only provides an easy way, and a hard way is flawed in the sense that it is a misguided explanation of the truth. What is correct is that life only offers us a right way and a wrong way. Those who understand this will most likely always accept the right way because they know most everything coming after will likely be easier. Those who don't understand will almost always choose the wrong way, believing it is easier to fear that they might someday be faced with what is hard instead of knowing it is already behind them.

There is a formula to a happy life consisting of four elements which must always be present. Everything begins with gratitude. Gratitude is the light which illuminates the darkness hiding all that we desire. It sheds light on the path to hope, which is the second element. Hope is what grows in the light once the darkness has been engulfed in the light, allowing for the nurturing of the third element, faith. Faith is what grows when we water with continued gratitude and warm the new growth with the light of the hope we create. And the three of these culminate into the fourth, prayer which is the action of sowing that which we plant in our lives. It is the ending action of believing the harvesting of gratitude, hope and faith is the certainty that our crops will provide a bounty beyond our expectations.

Choices are essentially building blocks. And we decide everything about those blocks. Their strength, appearance, dimensions, and texture. If what you are building is not the structure in which you envision, it may be time to choose different blocks.

Limitations are not conclusions, as they are subject to the winds of change and the circumstances which blow upon them. So, never allow a condition to become a definition, as this is giving control to that which it is not entitled to possess. Instead, embrace what fortune is blowing your way when you are against the wind, and allow it to sweep you from your burdens to a new unknown when it is at your back.

Be inspired today! Not by the accomplishments of others, but by what you have overcome. You have been dragged to the outer edges of hell, and still you believed enough to reach out to the heavens. You have been wronged, and yet you still chose what is right. When all hope seemed gone, you created it for yourself. And amid the chaos, you became the calm. The greatest of inspirations often come by persevering through the end of arduous defeats, even when giving in to the odds against you made the most sense.

Everything you learn, experience, and survive can bring about good and hope if you so choose. No matter how bad any situation seems, it only becomes a hopeless one if we accept it as one, or an enemy when we treat it as one. What we define takes on a living existence as that definition. So, choose wisely how you define each day in your life, because the power you afford the definitions you give them will become the authority that defines your entire life.

A martyr is always in control. Even when everything is out of control, they remain in control. Because they choose their destinies, they are free to travel any road, battle any enemy, and leave fear in the uncertainty where it belongs. This is because once we believe in anything enough to sacrifice wholeheartedly for it, any fear associated with it is replaced by a defiance to fail and a willingness to follow through that only resides on the fringes of existence.

If you allow someone else to think for you, then their thoughts will take hold while yours will wither. It will be their ideas which you cultivate, but your credit for their furtherance they will own. Do not follow those who expect control for themselves but accept guidance from those who teach you to own control of yourself. Giving up your direction to follow that of another leaves your journey a hollow void, never to be explored.

Conquerors amass lands. And yet the farmer gains more from the acre in which he eats. The wealthy amass fortunes they can never spend. And yet it is the poor who learn value as it is needed to survive. Tyrants rule over hordes, and yet the oppressed hearts rest not in servitude, but in freedom. Governments amass authority. But it is the people who own defiance, which does not answer to authority. Fulfillment comes not from what you acquire, but what you desire.

Close your eyes and remember a time in your life when you didn't feel fear. Think about the freedom you felt at that moment without the grip of something dark clutching your emotions. Think back on the simplicity without stress and a relief that seemed to surround you. Ponder a moment on the calmness that brought a sense of peace and calm in that moment. Now open your eyes and look at everything around you. What is that you see that has so much value, it's worth taking that feeling away from you?

At times in our lives, we are tasked with following, but never are we to accept where that will lead without questioning if the destination is the right direction for us. Often, we are only to follow until it leads us to a fork in the road. Just because someone leads you away from the fire does not mean they are leading you to safety.

The thing about creating a throwaway society is that you take away the importance of value. As such, you don't only throw away products, but eventually you end up throwing away people.

Pain is currency and that is how we pay our way through life. There is a price to life, a fee to experience both the good and the bad, the joyous and the sad. It's the cost to see the show. And in the end, if you assess the price was too high, then be assured that you focused so much on the cost of gaining entry that you missed the best parts of the show.

We were given a voice because evil will grow in silence. We were given language because unity requires communication and a lack of it divides us. We were given resolve because enemies are always determined. We were given the ability to listen because those against us boast of deeds. But above all these, we were given choice and that determines the amount of evil we are willing to accept.

When the rich want the poor to do better, that's hope. When the saved want salvation for all, that's faith. When the healthy want cures for the sick, that's compassion. When the poor refuse to steal from the rich, that's integrity. When the lost listen to the saved, that's trust. When the sick accept help from the healthy that's charity. Life always puts us on one side of the coin. And though we may not always have the option to flip the coin, we do have the power to give that coin more value.

———————

Purpose serves us, we do not serve it. When you understand this, you realize there are tasks in this life that only you can accomplish. Purpose guides you to those tasks. It shows you the value of them. And it never leaves you while completing them. And within each of them is the revelation that what you can accomplish and endure in this life was always hidden inside them.

———————

The force which pulls you is what keeps you on the right path. At times, it will be a negative one which is life telling you to fight and pull back. And other times, it will be positive telling you to stay the course and remain vigilant. But each force is needed to keep us from wandering aimlessly through life. This is because purpose lies in the narrowness of the middle. If we venture off course, purpose becomes misplaced. And your purpose may just be the door to someone else's path.

———————

If you ask as to the reason why evil exists in this world, consider that it was born out of the greatest notion in the universe-to be loved by choice. There is absolutely no requirement that someone love you. It is an action, possibly the only action, that is completely of free will. And it was worth taking the risk there would be such rampant evil; because even to the Creator, to be loved for no other reason than who you are, is the greatest knowledge in all creation.

We must all spend our time in hell. We must walk among the proverbial fire and brimstone existent upon the earth because it is the only situation in life where we learn the definition of peace. Circumstances which contain little, or no peace are the ones where we learn that our current damnation is actually peace, pushing us along the only road out of hell.

There are two things responsible for your happiness today, one is God, and the other is your choices. And if you choose not to believe in God, then you just chose one less reason to be happy.

The smallest spark can save us. Just a glimmer in the abyss can be a way out Remember that it is not the vast expense of the night sky we see when the shooting star glides across, but only the small flicker of light it emits. We are inherently drawn to the smallest of hopes no matter the size of despair surrounding us. This is to remind us that we are never forced accept the darkness regardless of the amount of light we can see.

The darkness we overcome becomes our property. It is defeated and no longer contains any control. As such, it becomes part of the arsenal which can be used to combat other dark forces in our lives. It is foolish to toss it to the past when it holds secrets that all negativities hold in common. Use the darkness, as it swallows what else is dark and eats it. It does so because it doesn't recognize its own when it's the light thrusting it in its direction.

Each despair you allow to defeat you becomes a weakness that is part of you, but the strengths you allow to overcome any weakness becomes all of you.

Never worry about fitting into someone else's category. Chances are, you won't fit in because you will find out that your place is exactly where you make it, and that categories only exist for those who haven't yet figured out their place.

There are so many things that I do not know. And many things I need to know. And a few things I don't want to know. And several things I wish I didn't know. And I am thankful for those things I don't know because I have no need to know. And of all the things there are to know, I realize true knowledge is knowing how to positively utilize what is known, and how to avoid what is best kept unknown.

Suffering without purpose is senseless. And often in life it seems our suffering is allowed when not warranted and without the understanding of a definitive purpose that allows us to make sense of it. And though unfair, there is nothing in the universe which hinders us from finding our own purpose. If we choose to do so, we gain a sense of control and direction in what is otherwise, beyond our control. We may not always have the power to change our surroundings or the coping skills to defeat it at that moment. But we do have the choice to assign meaning to anything that offers us the peace of mind purpose provides.

What is the value of one minute? Is its value in that we don't know how many we are given or is it in the expectation of what we can do with it? How we view that moment defines it. If we strive to change the world, all we need is a moment because we believe that possibility lives in every moment. If we wait until the last moment to see any value in it, then that moment just became the last possibility we will ever have.

The depths to which you are willing to travel directly correlates with how high you will rise. Not because of the distance you descend, but because those depths become comfortable and familiar making it easier to remain despite being mired in deceit. To rise to integrity and enlightenment allows only for descending enough to gain a foothold to climb but never deep enough to where it becomes easier to fall deeper than to reach upward.

If you expect help on your terms, then it's not help you want, but enabling. If you expect sympathy without the sacrifice of pride, then it's not sympathy you want, but pity. If you expect charity without an effort to improve your life circumstances, then it's not charity you seek, but a daily handout. If you expect forgiveness without a willingness to accept responsibility for actions, then it is not forgiveness you desire, but absolution without repentance. Because we expect something does not entitle us to define it as what we wish. That definition always belongs to the ones we ask to fulfil those expectations.

One of the greatest misconceptions is that there is only weakness in the darkness. In our despair and depression, we are often told there is only hope that we will make it to the light, leaving us to believe there is nothing else in the darkness. In truth, everything is still there, just not visible in the darkness. Strength, courage, conviction, and hope are all present, but instead of being seen with the eyes, they must be felt by the heart.

If you're standing in the darkness, it does not matter how close you are to the light. If your back is turned to it, you will not see it. Never allow your perspective to be your only guide. For its focus may only be what the eyes see and not the possibilities the heart knows.

THE END

To keep up with new quotes, please visit
www.uniquelahoma.com